CELEBRATING THE CITY OF DENPASAR

Celebrating the City of Denpasar

Walter the Educator

Silent King Books

SILENT KING BOOKS

SKB

Copyright © 2024 by Walter the Educator

All rights reserved. No part of this book may be reproduced in any manner whatsoever without written permission except in the case of brief quotations embodied in critical articles and reviews.

First Printing, 2024

Disclaimer
This book is a literary work; the story is not about specific persons, locations, situations, and/or circumstances unless mentioned in a historical context. Any resemblance to real persons, locations, situations, and/or circumstances is coincidental. This book is for entertainment and informational purposes only. The author and publisher offer this information without warranties expressed or implied. No matter the grounds, neither the author nor the publisher will be accountable for any losses, injuries, or other damages caused by the reader's use of this book. The use of this book acknowledges an understanding and acceptance of this disclaimer.

Celebrating the City of Denpasar is a little collectible souvenir book that belongs to the Celebrating Cities Book Series by Walter the Educator. Collect them all and more books at WaltertheEducator.com

USE THE EXTRA SPACE TO TAKE NOTES AND DOCUMENT YOUR MEMORIES

DENPASAR

In the heart of the emerald archipelago,

Celebrating the City of
Denpasar

Where the gods once danced in the whispers of the sea,

Lies Denpasar, a city where time flows,

Like the ancient rhythms of the gamelan symphony.

Streets adorned with vibrant tapestries,

Of markets bustling with fragrant wares,

Where the artisans' hands weave histories,

Celebrating the City of
Denpasar

Into batik patterns, intricate and rare.

Under the canopy of tropical skies,

Temples rise, their stone faces serene,

Guardians of secrets, where offerings lie,

In lotus blooms and incense dreams.

Denpasar's pulse is a heartbeat strong,

Echoing through rice fields, lush and green,

Where farmers sing their timeless songs,

And kites soar high in the afternoon gleam.

Here, the past and present intertwine,

In a dance as fluid as the ocean's tide,

Celebrating the City of
Denpasar

Where ancient chants in Balinese align,

With modern beats, a citywide guide.

By the sacred river, where myths reside,

Children play in the sun's golden light,

Their laughter mingles with the tide,

In a melody that feels just right.

The scent of frangipani fills the air,

As twilight paints the horizon's edge,

Denpasar breathes a beauty rare,

Celebrating the City of
Denpasar

A living canvas, a sacred pledge.

Beneath the banyan tree's wise embrace,

Elders gather, sharing tales of old,

Their stories weave a communal grace,

In words like threads spun in gold.

Markets hum with a vibrant song,

Of spices, fruits, and treasures galore,

From dawn till dusk, the throngs belong,

In this kaleidoscope of culture and lore.

Denpasar's nights are a symphony,

Of cicadas' serenades and temple gongs,

Lanterns glow, a luminous decree,

Guiding wayfarers with ancient songs.

Celebrating the City of
Denpasar

ABOUT THE CREATOR

Walter the Educator is one of the pseudonyms for Walter Anderson. Formally educated in Chemistry, Business, and Education, he is an educator, an author, a diverse entrepreneur, and he is the son of a disabled war veteran. "Walter the Educator" shares his time between educating and creating. He holds interests and owns several creative projects that entertain, enlighten, enhance, and educate, hoping to inspire and motivate you.

Follow, find new works, and stay up to date with Walter the Educator™
at WaltertheEducator.com

www.ingramcontent.com/pod-product-compliance
Lightning Source LLC
LaVergne TN
LVHW052007060526
838201LV00059B/3896